Man in the Long Grass
cricket poems

David Phillips

foreword by Mike Selvey

First published November 2001 by
IRON Press
5, Marden Tce
Cullercoats
Northumberland
NE30 4PD
England
Tel: 0191 253 1901
e-mail: seaboy@freenetname.co.uk
web site: www.ironpress.co.uk

Typeset in Trebuchet MS 12pt
Printed by Peterson Printers, South Shields, England
© Copyright individual poems David Phillips 2001
© Copyright this edition, IRON Press 2001

Book and cover design by IRON Eye @ Iron Press

ISBN 0 906228 82 4

IRON Press are represented by
Signature Book Representation
Sun House, 2 Little Peter Street
Manchester M15 4PS
England
Tel: 0161 834 8767
e-mail: admin@signature-books.co.uk

SUPPORTED BY
THE NATIONAL LOTTERY
THROUGH
THE **ARTS COUNCIL**
OF ENGLAND

Dedicated to the memory of my father

David Phillips has had poems published in a variety of magazines including the *Spectator*, *New Statesman*, *Poetry Review* and *IRON Magazine*. He has had two plays broadcast on radio and won a number of competitions, including a £1000 first prize in a bun-fight refereed by *The Poetry Society*.

Contents

- 6 Foreword by Mike Selvey
- 9 Running on Empty
- 12 Caught
- 13 Heavy Roller
- 14 14th April
- 15 Spells
- 17 Pyjama Pickle
- 19 Vanishing Act
- 20 Unfair Prayer
- 21 Within a Budding Grove
- 23 The Rasumovsky Quartets
- 24 Suzanne
- 27 Twelve
- 28 Nightwatchman
- 30 Church Lane End
- 31 Harvestman
- 33 Champers Match
- 34 A Framed Photo Discovered Hanging in the Chairman's Lavatory
- 36 Test Non-Selection
- 38 After a Shock Defeat to a Minor County Side
- 39 Jenkins
- 41 Autographs
- 42 Slogarithms
- 44 Somewhere Else
- 45 Goodyear
- 46 Hospitality Boxes
- 48 Man in the Long Grass
- 49 Landscape with Figures
- 52 Dusty
- 54 Chinese Cricket
- 56 Neck and Crop
- 58 Butterfingers
- 60 Dropped
- 62 Old Nemesis
- 65 Twelfth Man
- 67 CCC
- 68 No Such Thing as a Bad Hundred
- 71 Spiteful
- 72 Over the Top
- 75 Like Shelling Peas
- 77 Over
- 80 Batman
- 82 Theatre in the Round
- 84 Happy Endings
- 86 26 September

Foreword

by Mike Selvey

Does, or did David Phillips play cricket? Personally, I haven't a clue. *Wisden* tells me (and who is to dispute it?) that H. Phillips played for Sussex - although as he died in 1919 we can probably discount him - and that three further Phillips R.B., W.B., and W.N., all played state cricket in Australia. But no Phillips D. So it doesn't look like first-class cricket is in his CV. Good club standard perhaps, although it doesn't really matter either way. The point is that his poems genuinely read as if he's been there, done it and cried the tears not as a star with the sponsored Merc, but as a spearchucker who never quite hacks it.

This, I might say, is a rarity, for if cricket, because of the infinite variety of its nature, attracts quality writing in a quantity that no other sport can match, then it also becomes a vehicle for over-romanticising. In cricket fantasy land it is always sunny, crowds snooze in deckchairs, the rhododendrons are out at Tunbridge Wells, and some rapier-bladed D'Artagnan of the willow has caressed the crimson rambler all over the greensward and is acknowledging applause like a rain shower on a tin roof for a sublime century. Even John Betjeman (whose *Collected Poems* accompany me everywhere, and whose pre-eminence I will concede to no-one, not even Phillip Larkin) was at it in his poem *Cheltenham* where, *"I composed these lines when a Summer wind/ was blowing the elm leaves dry/ and we were seventy-six for seven/ and they had C.B.Fry"*.(And we were in the shit, by the sound of it). No-one talks of helmets or pissing rain, or bones broken by pace barrages, or a shortleg fielder asking who is shagging the batsman's missus while he is on his away trip.

Now I think this is because the vast majority of cricket's literature is written from the standpoint of the spectator and maybe they do want to dream a little, for what is the point of creating sporting heroes if they cannot then be placed on a pedestal? From within the game though there is a different story to tell and David Phillips manages it. These are poems with which players will identify. *14 April* for example, that ridiculous time when the season starts and you swaddle in long johns and sweaters for a finger numbing session in the field, longing for the interval only to find a bloody salad lunch waiting.

Reminds me of Derby or John Jameson clubbing it around the Courtaulds ground at Coventry, And read here the poem *Dropped*. It certainly happened to me and I recall my anger at the injustice, as I perceived it, and my scorn for the captain's new toy. Rejection is a hard thing to handle at any level and few, I reckon, if they really care, are able to take it with equanimity. Not me for sure.

Dropped might have been written for me: *"Though bile makes a bitter cup/ I can't but hope they fuck it up"*. Shameful but true.

Mike Selvey is cricketing correspondent for **The Guardian**.

RUNNING ON EMPTY

At the end of September they give me the shove,
a steep plunge in profits has stricken the Board,
the club is in crisis; the fat has to go,
the Chairman sees me as a starter for slimming:
so sorry, but cricket's a business, old boy -
there's all sorts of angles and all kinds of reasons,
but thanks for the previous twenty-three seasons.

I hadn't enjoyed the brightest of summers:
a hamstring in April was not a good start,
the weather was dreadful in June and July,
some umpiring calls I could hardly believe,
and the captain could never decide where to play me.
It seemed that my batting was devilled by fate -

but most of the time I wasn't that great.

What can I say? I'd a run of cheap scores
but was I washed up as a County player?
Everyone thought so; nobody batted
an eye when I got my cards at the close
and a silver salver with the wrong dates engraved.
So I cleaned out the locker and left my address,
farewell to celebrity, hello DSS.

And then the overseas signing fell through,
our all-rounder was banned for unauthorised drugs,

and the opening bat was poached by TV.
So suddenly there on the mat, a new contract
with a grovelling note from the Chairman's PA.
But do I need all the blood, sweat and pain -
and can I face that dressing-room again?

CAUGHT

Another world - my first class debut:
14 runs, caught Flower, bowled Skinner.
Team photograph: Jeeze, I'm three stone slimmer!

Stand like a broom with a cricket bat,
face so white it's positively see-through;
look to need a damn good dinner.

Made up for things since then of course - in spades,
you'd think the sporting life would keep me slender,
but years of puds and pints don't make you thinner.

Time plays its cruellest jest on fey young men,
while cricket gods who run to fat are shades
who startle with their ghastly splendour.

HEAVY ROLLER

Too huge to enclose at the end of September,
it's left by the sight-screen and covered with sheeting,
abandoned to the frosts and snows of December.

Long winter months drag, but at last in spring time
the tarpaulin's untied, hauled off, releasing
a six-ton behemoth clagged with rust and grime.

The County ground staff set to make it brighter
with oil, emery cloth and elbow greasing;
each April actually making it slightly lighter.

14 APRIL

Counted on the fingers of three hands
a crowd wrapped up for winter in the stands
applaud us into summer as we're blown
by gusting April winds which bite the bone.

And daffodils wave by the betting tent,
an outstayed welcome in this endless lent;
horse-chestnut buds keep resolutely sealed
as fifteen men stand shivering in a field.

Until at last it's lunchtime; chapped with cold
we stagger up the steps and lunch is doled
by ladies who think cricket meals a breeze:
cold ham salad, ice cream, iced tea, hard cheese.

SPELLS

Sometimes I'm called upon to turn my arm
when partnerships prolong beyond their due,
the skipper feels it can't do any harm
and I could be the one to split the pair
and make a monkey out of No.1 or 2.

My bowling spell at times is cruelly brief,
I'm sharpish but if batsmen get my pitch
the ploy of using me may end in grief
with balls deposited among the crowd
engendering a rapid bowling switch.

But sometimes when I'm asked to take the ball
a little magic comes along as well:

I see a batsman heading for a fall,
too weak, too clumsy to resist; he plays,
he slips, he stumbles - helpless in my spell.

PYJAMA PICKLE

For playing in the one day game
I have to wear pyjamas with my name
emblazoned on the back so punters
know their Olive Oyls from Billy Bunters.

And stunning is my suit of green,
in play-school it would make the scene,
but I play for a pickle co.
whose range of products everyone must know:
horse-radish, scotch egg, gherkin, saveloy -
I bat and bowl in their employ.

I think the hype and razzmatazz
demeans the game and all their gear has

made me look not up-to-date and cool
but reinforced the archetypal flannelled fool.
Call me stuck-up and call me fickle
but I hate playing as a pickle.

VANISHING ACT

The thinnest of margins,
a shadow of doubt,
one moment you're in,
next moment you're out.

You play like an angel,
you slay the attack,
you run like a hare,
now you're marching back.

So how has this happened
and why are you here?
What terrible magic
made you disappear?

UNFAIR PRAYER

I'm 30 not out when they bring on their quickie,
a gigantic Jamaican all scowling and mean,
he looks like a heavy-weight bouncer or bruiser -
a 240-pound killing machine.

He marks out his run-up in seven league strides,
has a practice charge-in and turns back again;
he waits for a moment then undoes his shirt
and reverently kisses a cross on a chain.

I glare back at him and prepare for a snorter,
and wonder why pacemen need God's help this way;
and if I myself now offer a prayer
will it cancel his out, thus restoring fair play?

WITHIN A BUDDING GROVE

Late April and the first downpour;
the ground's a patchy grey lake
and men with long wide brooms
are pushing water at each other.

It's thought a start could be made
by half-past three this afternoon,
which means I have to hang about.
And it's *still* raining.

I'd like to play some cricket
but feet up on the balcony
with a fag, a cup of tea and Proust
I would say is the next best thing.

A nattily blazered Chairman approaches
the paint-flaked balcony rail,
puts his fat fingers into the rain,
ignores me completely and goes back again.

Inside the dressing-room the telly's on,
and Monopoly cards are being shuffled;
a *Sun* is contemptuously tossed aside
and a *Star* hauled up from the floor.

I'd quite like a game of Monopoly
but no one invites me inside to play.
How Marcel would have laughed at cricket!
They can take their sodding game and stick it.

THE RASUMOVSKY QUARTETS

When batting you must concentrate the mind,
shoo every pure and impure thought away;
a catchy tune looped in the head I find
allows the brain to focus on each ball
                              and helps me play.

Don't need at all to be a highbrow cheese
for any nagging phrase will serve to milk
the bowling, and patently this useful wheeze
makes no distinction between Beethoven
                              and Acker Bilk.

SUZANNE

You ask if my wife comes to watch me play?
When we first got together she thought it was great
that I played in the League and might play for the County one day.

She came to the matches, palled up with the blokes
and helped the girls with the lunches and teas
and ironed my kit (which was one of our jokes).

When I signed for the County and cash seemed less tight
we got married and moved to a house near the ground.
We were happy then and our life was . . . well, all right.

We started a family - both wanted kids,

David Phillips

I thought I could juggle my home and my job,
but my love for the game put our love on the skids.

Too often away fixtures did nothing to fix
a relationship glued in resentment and pain -
she wanted a Joe who would come home at six.

She thought I was stupid to stay in a game
which loved you or hated you, dropped you at will,
favoured the lucky and gifted the same.

And I felt the pressure of having to give
a 100% for my place in the team
as home life grew tougher, less rewarding to live.

We split up last Christmas, agreed not to tell;
I still see the kids and we play out a game
to convince everyone we're as happy as hell.

You ask if my wife comes to watch me play?
I do send her tickets but she never comes -
cricket's a dull game when love's gone away.

TWELVE

The umpire suddenly stops the game,
we've twelve men fielding instead of eleven.
The captain pointedly counts us all: eleven.
The umpire counts us again: twelve.
We all count each other: eleven.
The umpire says forget it and play on.

Ten minutes later he stops us again,
we've twelve men fielding and one must go.
The captain calls us up and lines us up:
one-two-three-four-five-six-seven-eight-nine-ten-ELEVEN!
And what about HIM? The umpire says,
pointing at the dark beneath the trees.

NIGHTWATCHMAN

Last ball to face
and common sense suggests
it would be nice
to start again
with wicket safe,
runs on the board,
a good night's sleep
and everything to play for
in the morning.

And everybody thinks
a dot-ball's on the cards:
spectators leave,
man in the deep inclines

towards pavilion gate
and stewards stoop
to draw the covers on.
And do I thrash it?
Nope, I block away
and live to fail another day.

CHURCH LANE END

Superb to see that slender spire
pierce through the billowed chestnut choir,
pink blossom splashed on railway green
as in a *Rupert Annual* scene.

The spire points up to the sky
and that is where some batsmen try
to drive the ball, though not one strike
has ever found that iron spike.

But still we hope to bang the slats
and wake the hanging belfry bats,
or loose into the graves a thwack
where none will rise to chuck it back.

HARVESTMAN

Nine, ten, jack to come
with thirty runs required to win,
my contribution to this sum
expected to be high,
the wicket taking spin,
the rabbits wild of eye,
it's down to me to galvanise the scrum
so don't forget the fruit gum, chum.

And I farm all the strike I can -
pinch singles as the over ends,
give nothing to the other man
that might advance a wicket
and bring his bunny friends.

THE VANITY OF CRICKET!
With two to make and the game in the can
I'm caught myself, which wasn't quite the plan.

CHAMPERS MATCH

In June our Chairman lays on steaks and beer
and lets the players roam his country pile,
(to see how much we've made him through the year)
I joke too loudly, catch his icy smile.

And yes, there's cricket on the lawn; I pad
six runs then give an easy caught and bowled.
The ten-year old's delighted - so's his dad -
'Well played!' Sir says, and fills my glass with gold.

A FRAMED PHOTOGRAPH DISCOVERED HANGING IN THE CHAIRMAN'S LAVATORY

The mottled photo shows a locomotive
pitched through a station's windows
into the street below. Leaning at forty-five
degrees, the truck and tender climb
down perilously from a vast archway.

Masonry and window frame make sharp shadows
across an early morning pavement. It doesn't say
if anyone was standing underneath at the time.

Incongruous deaths at first raise nervous laughs -
the thought of someone flattened by a falling train.
But then it's odd how unexpected ends can pain

those left to look at long-snapped photographs.

Please God, surprise me with a death that's merciful,
like the Lord's sparrow struck by a cricket ball.

TEST NON-SELECTION

Never had a decent game
when Illy came
to watch me play.

And what Ted Dexter saw
was really poor,
I have to say.

And David Gower
watched a rotten hour
when I batted like a prat.

Athers saw me give a show
but that was years ago

and he's forgotten that.

Stewart watched me make a ton
then picked his son -
that set *him* rolling.

Then there was Mike Gatting
but I wasn't even batting
and he never cared much for my bowling.

AFTER A SHOCK DEFEAT TO A MINOR COUNTY SIDE

There is a green field far away
  without a stand or wall,
Where our dear team was crucified -
  four crashed off my last ball.

JENKINS

Our club accountant, Hubert Jenkins
died in 1923;
found at his roll-top watching play
as Hammond torched us after tea.

A thrill too far, the heart gave way
as Wally edged a chance to Stroud;
the catch put down the Master put
the next four balls into the crowd.

And since that time a ghost has walked,
or not walked, since he's always there
with white-washed face glued to the window,
goldfish mouthing, bug-eyed stare.

Though I've not seen him, others claim
to feel a presence in that room
where he scratched the County's ledgers,
now a home for pale and broom.

But what a wonder it would be
to feel old Jenkins' fetid breath;
if Hubert lives he gives us all
eternal life - the death of Death.

AUTOGRAPHS

It used to be schoolboys with ink on the sleeve
who'd wait in the car park and pounce when you'd leave
with their programmes and books and photos to sign.

But now a young player may chance on a line
of pubescent schoolgirls who ambush their star
leaving kisses and numbers all over his car.

SLOGARITHMS

Your tail-end charley's numerate and bright,
his foolproof wheeze to best the pace attack
providing insight for the connoisseur
in how to cope with bowling that shows spite.

Of six balls in the over, say, number two
he deems is going to be the one to smack
with all the others blocked or left alone,
temptation reigned in for one great yahoo.

It's simple really but a question begs:
balls three or five might be the ones to crack
with number two the worst one of the bunch.
Dismiss pedantic thoughts - this scheme has legs.

A *batsman* judges each ball as it's bowled,
attack/defence it's all down to his choice;
but if you sideline five balls out of six
you concentrate the mind, give only gold.

You also put the bowler off his stroke,
how can he tell what ball you're going to bang?
With one in six you play the numbers game,
excite the crowd, and make the pacemen choke.

SOMEWHERE ELSE

Players in the dressing-room
lolling round the set,
watching Dutch League football,
how selfish can you get?

Outside the tail is struggling,
the quicks unleashed make free
with fiery, spiteful bowling
as our batsmen watch TV.

GOODYEAR

An airship floats above the stands;
we stop and stare and wonder
why anything so ancient should appear,
a whirring wraith from quite another era.

Above the match they must look down
and see a ritual from a *Movietone*:
Hobbs and Hammond's ghostly figures
turning in an endless summer.

HOSPITALITY BOXES

I watch those sods sip G & T,
late cut a ball and scamper two,
but then they have their backs to me
like red-arsed monkeys in a zoo,
these business geeks are bloody rude.

What actor on a stage would play
before ill-mannered oiks like these?
For every player worth his pay
is driven by the need to please
with something given in return.

The Chairman says they bring in loot;
I think indifference breeds disdain,

and if an arsehole in a suit
wants corporate junkets let him drain
his Bolly glass elsewhere I say.

I miss a straight one, there's a sound
of thudded pad below the knee,
but in the boxes round the ground
men still stand with their backs to me
and miss what they might like to see.

MAN IN THE LONG GRASS

I used to be thought of as sharp in the slips,
my eye and reaction time swift as a spell;
I did pouch some sitters and missed a few pips
but snapped a fair number of blinders as well.

And punters would come just to wait for the catches
that flew to my hands as if guided by God;
the Chairman would say that my fielding won matches
and Man of the Match judges gave me the nod.

But now without telling me Time has arranged
for my skill and my quickness of thinking to sleep,
and far from the slips my position has changed,
I'm out in the long grass and lost in the deep.

LANDSCAPE WITH FIGURES

Within the borders of her imagined frame
an artist sees the summer game,
a canvas long in white and green
commissioned by *The Perfect Pickle Co.*
to place the County team on show.

The painting comes on slowly day by day
although the action's stilled in play -
throughout a four day game is seen
a single moment which her art
decides has frozen summer's heart.

And in the foreground grinning down,
I stand, a half-wit cricket clown,

perhaps the kind of man I might have been.
Unrepresentative? She laughs,
if you think art is life take photographs.

I say at least photography is real
and shows the way that people are and feel,
it's always clear what snapshots mean;
an artist has a duty too
to look at me and paint what's true.

She shrugs and smiles and dips her brush again
to make the change that makes me sane,
a small amendment to the scene
that satisfies a drawing bore

(the match ends in a boring draw).

In years to come when dust and grime
have sealed these painted men in time,
their lives and reputations pickled clean,
an idle glance may possibly wonder why
one flannelled fool up there appears to cry.

DUSTY

For eighty years as boy and man
I've watched my team play on this ground,
I saw the good and great come here;
an epoch passed within my span,
the Golden Age of cricket wound
itself around my member's chair.

And now I've gone I wish my dust
be scattered on the Church Lane crease
where Collins, Howarth, Wentworth, Roe,
Purcell, Dubarry, Truscott, Crust
took strike and made the world's woes cease
in perfect summers long ago.

Not nice for us who'd have to bat
in human ash if ground staff chose
to take requests like these as read -
it's swept beneath the junior's mat.
No disrespect of course to those
who miss the point of being dead.

CHINESE CRICKET

The *chinaman* and *chinese cut*, so coined
when 'trick' was deemed analogous to 'chink'
for any gambit that seemed odd
by cricketers not paid to think
and half the world was British Empire pink.

And Peking might have been a Martian moon
for all your English county player knew,
both Eaton toff and yeoman batter
connived in ignorance that grew
into a game appealing to so few.

The Chinese would I think be good at cricket,
stamp the sport with their own playing style,

find some aspect they'd excel at,
grace the game with speed and guile,
compete and no doubt stuff us by a mile.

NECK AND CROP

I stand in shock, bowled neck and crop,
the wicket splayed out like a fan.
Oh God, another bloody flop.

The fielders run to hug their man;
incomprehensibly I stay
as if the verdict somehow was in doubt.

A pause too long, the keeper has his say,
Piss off, you silly cunt, you're fucking out!

The long trudge back, and in my head
a replay like an inquest for the dead:

David Phillips

I saw the ball drift slowly from the hand,
I traced the curve, I watched the bugger land,
I raised my bat to let it pass,
it spread my stumps and left me standing like an arse.

BUTTERFINGERS

I field far out in the deep
and talk to a girl in a hat,
she's on holiday here with her grandma and granddad,
he's crackers about cricket.
Whoops, there goes another wicket.

The old boy's fallen asleep
which gives me a chance for a chat,
you'd like to see more of the place? I'm so glad,
they do a terrific steak
at the Inn on the Lake.

A ball hit long and steep
follows me like a cat.

I spill the catch and the hopes I had.
Her sympathetic smiles
show me I missed by miles.

DROPPED

Dropped from the team,
I dropped a catch
the Chairman claimed
lost us the match.

I don't see how
one man can bin
a game which ten
have failed to win.

And nothing's said
and no one's stopped
to say they're sorry
I've been dropped.

But there's the team list
and my name
is absent from
tomorrow's game.

Though bile makes
a bitter cup
I can't but hope
they fuck it up.

OLD NEMISIS

A short announcement through the Tannoy,
the crowd's blank faces tell his story,
forgotten far beyond their caring
but in his pomp he had them roaring.

He'd stride out capless, shirt cuffs flapping;
bat, a bludgeon (crimson showing
where the sweet spot made a circle)
he cut and sliced like any surgeon.

Twelve quid a week were all the commons
that his art could then command;
a fruit drink advert on the telly
took our snobby breaths away.

But when his playing days were over
the ads stopped too, the cricket lover
once again could bask in rapture
at the fag-card hero picture.

Then some grim lines in the *Mirror*
told us of his court case horror:
three months inside, sentence suspended
in view of an unblemished record.

Unblemished in the writ of *Wisden*,
his fame and honour there are certain;
no single shotgun blast can savage
those brave and splendid cricket pages.

He played too marvellous a sport;
when golden youth and fame depart
the later years have little left
to counterweight an end so swift.

And as the crowd mill at the gates
they leave behind newspaper hats,
and there amidst the hype and lies,
a three-line squib: *Test Player Dies*.

TWELFTH MAN

Falling asleep in a chair in the sun,
detached from the game, unimpressed by the play;
a clack of the ball and a scampering run
the only distractions - we're losing (hooray!)

Stretched out on the balcony, boots on the rail,
the lounger reclined, the *Silk Cut* out;
this is the sentence for daring to fail,
they give you your money for arsing about.

The lad who took over from me gets a duck,
shouldered arms at a straight one that cannoned his knee;
of course you could say it's a bit of bad luck,
but bad luck for him must be good luck for me.

The skipper and Chairman sit huddled and glum,
let's try Plan B and rejig all the places;
and is that a glance at the discarded bum?
It's quite hard to tell with egg on their faces.

Perhaps they'll relent and forgive me, who knows?
Before I can wonder what anyone thinks
a jockstrap is dangled in front of my nose -
it's time for the twelfth man to carry the drinks.

C.C.C

What is a County Cricket Club?
The bricks, the walls, the stands, the pitch?
The members, players, groundsmen, staff?
The shareholders, the Chairman's 51%?

Perhaps the name that swings above a pub?
The farmer's land once portioned by a ditch?
The glaze of sepia on a photograph
where yeoman pro takes strike with Harrow gent?

I watched the captain tearing off a cub
for acting though he owned the place. That's rich
from someone who gets parking space for half
a dozen cars. I wonder what he meant?

NO SUCH THING AS A BAD HUNDRED

Off the mark;
the greatest innings
always start from small beginnings.

Ten runs;
double figures in my score,
from where they came there's plenty more.

Twenty runs;
well, I can say
I made more than the boss today.

Thirty runs;
no one can shout

if I now get myself out.

Forty runs;
would please most men,
but I would like another ten.

Fifty runs;
the crowd applaud
the big five-o up on the board.

Sixty runs;
this season's best,
let's see if I can make the rest.

Seventy runs;
the singles flow,
only three more tens to go.

Eighty runs;
I'm steaming on,
surprised that all my nerves have gone.

Ninety runs;
they've all come back,
I push, I prod, I poke, I hack.

A century!
I raise my bat,
now let the buggers chew on that.

SPITEFUL

I find an extra yard of pace
and dig one in, the ball jags up
and whacks the batsman in the face.

Poleaxed, he steps back on his wicket,
blood on his cheek, the field goes up,
the howl is answered. Well, that's cricket!

And no one says what a shit I am;
a mob of grinning apes run up
as if I didn't give a damn.

OVER THE TOP

This touring side has got the lot:
batsmen, bowlers, fielding stars,
the magic balls, the magic bats,
they've flattened every county side
and won three test games on the trot;
but like brave soldiers we aspire
to win our DSO's and bars.

Our captain's talk is all Dunkirk,
his phiz a mask of studied gloom
which since we haven't faced a ball
has blown our nerve before we start.
We really need to lose this berk
if his gee-up's going to be

the biggest downer since Khartoum.

We lose the toss and get put in,
the skipper thinks he'll bat at six
instead of opening the knock
and sends me out to blunt the steel.
It's actually not too bad - I thin
the slips with several hefty whacks
and make a few before they spread my sticks.

And things work out - we pinch a draw,
some helpful rain steals half a day,
their pacemen find our pitch too slow,
the fusillade falls short and wide.

Our captain makes the highest score,
there seems to be a moral here
but what it is I really couldn't say.

LIKE SHELLING PEAS

Cricket's an easy game
when you're young.

When you're young
you don't really think.

You don't really think
you'll get old one day.

You'll get old one day,
you won't even notice.

You won't even notice
when the magic leaves you.

When the magic leaves you
technique is everything.

Technique is everything
you tell everyone.

You tell everyone,
everyone says it's true.

Everyone says it's true,
cricket's an easy game.

OVER

Stand in the shadow
then out of the shadow.

Sun too low to dazzle
game too slow to dazzle.

Advance for the bowling,
retreat for the blocking.

Stand in the shadow
then out of the shadow.

Stare at the scoreboard,
stare at the scoreboard clock.

Is there death after cricket,
is there cricket after death?

Talk to a girl in the crowd
and bore a girl in the crowd.

Sign somebody's programme
then read somebody's programme.

Stand in the shadow
then out of the shadow.

I would have a wicket if I could get the ball,
I would have a ball if I could get a wicket.

Try to catch the captain's eye,
fail to catch the captain's eye.

Stand in the shadow
then out of the shadow.

Think about Sue and the kids,
and think about Sue and the kids.

Stand in the shadow
then out of the shadow.

Stand in the shadow
then out of the shadow.

BATMAN

At school I really wasn't very good,
picked for my bowling rather than the batting;
old Mr Barks, the coach, saw me make a ton
but that was indoors on coconut matting,
and if I only swung the bat for fun
I certainly took my bowling as seriously as I could.

A rotten snob, I thought spin bowling posh,
read and re-read Richie Benaud's bible-book,
and Barksie helped me with my line and length.
But schoolboy batsmen love to drive and hook;
consistency was not my greatest strength -
I often took the field with jugs of squash.

In one school match when I was batting No. 7
with the game already lost, instead of slogging
everything in sight I decided just to stay in,
keep my wicket intact and concentrate on jogging
the score along - not get out, not try to win.
I stayed forever and found a kind of cricket heaven.

I realised it was concentration that made me good,
relished the supreme challenge of being on my own,
one man against eleven, all of who wanted me gone.
With that single innings a potent seed was sown,
a batsman I would be from now on,
my whole life focussed on a yard of wood.

THEATRE IN THE ROUND

Cricket's better than theatre,
it's less pretentious and the people are earthier;
you've got your cast of accomplished players:
king roles, large parts, small parts, walk-ons,
everyone knows exactly what they have to do,
how they must perform, the correct order of things,
But no one knows how anything will turn out!

In some ways the game's more akin to opera -
long stretches of almost unbelievable boredom
punctuated by brief flashes of paroxysmal excitement.
Naturally the exciting bits wouldn't be so exciting
if they weren't flanked by the long boring bits.
These are usually provided by *prima donnas* who swan

about trying to convince us how marvellous they are.

And then you have the old stagers like me:
not in any sense a star but no spear carrier either;
we do our best and you couldn't do without us,
but no one sticks our pictures up on their walls;
we are the meat and potatoes and gravy men,
the six, seven, eight, nine, ten men who skulk around
the dressing room plotting *how to steal the show!*

HAPPY ENDINGS

An unexceptional trophy, *but we won!*
It's big, it's gold, it's ours and that's what matters,
a great result for all the hard work done
by fans and staff, fielders, bowlers, batters.

To lift the match award for me was sweet,
a bright and breezy not-out 58
saw victory snatched from certain defeat
(and some had humble pie slapped on their plate).

But that's all in the past, the Chairman's here
with popping fizz to blow away the pain;
my hair's shampooed with Krug instead of beer,
though what a waste of bloody good champagne!

And from the pages of tomorrow's press
I'll cut and paste the story of my fame,
and read the bullshit as the hacks confess
to sadness at my giving up the game.

26 SEPTEMBER

The fielders wait,
the air is summer sweet,
the afternoon as warm as June,
the fixture list complete,
the end has come too soon.

An autumn sun dips low,
a season's gold
lies swept in leafy heaps,
the last ball is bowled,
and cricket sleeps.

IRON Press has been championing new writing since 1973, and is as committed as ever to the principles of small press publishing. We spurn literary competitions, marketing junkets or overhyped hacks, while continuing our policy of discovering the best new talent in the North-East region, the rest of the country and sometimes the world.

We bring out four or five new titles a year- single collections of poetry and fiction, international anthologies and contemporary plays.

If you would like a copy of our booklist
please contact us by snail mail, email or phone
and don't forget to visit our website.

**IRON Press
5 Marden Terrace, Cullercoats
North Shields, Northumberland NE30 4PD, UK
Tel/Fax: 0191 253 1901
E-mail: seaboy@freenetname.co.uk
website: www.ironpress.co.uk**